ANIMALS

Spiders

by Kevin J. Holmes

Content Consultant:
Spider Bob Breene
The American Tarantula Society

Bridgestone Books

an imprint of Capstone Press

Bridgestone Books are published by Capstone Press
818 North Willow Street, Mankato, Minnesota 56001
http://www.capstone-press.com

Library of Congress Cataloging-in-Publication Data
Holmes, Kevin J.
    Spiders/by Kevin J. Holmes.
    p. cm.--(Animals)
    Includes bibliographical references (p. 23) and index.
    Summary: An introduction to spiders' physical characteristics, habits, prey, and
relationships to human beings.
    ISBN 1-56065-605-0
    1. Spiders--Juvenile literature. [1. Spiders.] I. Title.
II. Series: Animals (Mankato, Minn.)
QL458.4.H645   1998
595.4′4--dc21

                                                        97-11966
                                                          CIP
                                                           AC

Photo credits
Root Resources/Anthony Mercieca, 8, 14, 20
James P. Rowan, cover, 4, 6, 10
Unicorn Stock/Ron Partis, 12; A. Gurmankin, 16; Dede Gilman, 18

Table of Contents

Legs

Spinnerets

Abdomen

Cephalothorax

Eyes

Fangs

Fast Facts

Kinds: There are about 36,000 kinds of spiders. Scientists find more kinds every year.

Range: Spiders live almost everywhere on earth.

Habitat: Spiders live in forests, plains, mountains, deserts, and underwater.

Food: Most spiders eat insects. Some eat small fish or frogs. Large spiders may eat smaller spiders.

Mating: Many spiders mate in the summer or fall. Some mate anytime.

Young: Young spiders are called spiderlings. They hatch from eggs.

Spiders

Spiders are arthropods. An arthropod is an animal with a hard outer shell. Arthropods have many legs with joints. A joint is a place where two parts meet. Many people think that spiders are insects. But they are not insects.

All spiders have similar bodies. They have two main body parts. They have eight legs. Most spiders have eight eyes. But some have as many as 24. Others do not have any eyes.

Spiders are predators. A predator is an animal that hunts other animals for food.

Scientists have discovered about 36,000 kinds of spiders. Scientists believe there may be as many as 170,000 kinds. Scientists find more kinds of spiders every year.

Most spiders have eight eyes.

Appearance

Spiders can be almost every color. Some are black. Others are pink. Still others are yellow. Some have long hair. Others have short hair.

Spiders can be different sizes also. Some are as big as three and one-half inches (nine centimeters). Others are as small as a pinhead.

The front part of a spider's body is called the cephalothorax. The eyes, the mouth, and the legs are part of this section. Next to a spider's mouth are two large fangs. A spider releases poison through these fangs.

The back part of a spider's body is called the abdomen. It is usually large and round. This part of the body makes the spider's silk. Silk is a sticky string made in a spider's body. The silk comes out of the abdomen through openings. These openings are called spinnerets.

Spiders can be almost every color.

Homes

Some spiders make silk webs for homes. Different kinds of spiders build different kinds of webs. The orbweaver spider's webs look like circles. The triangle spider builds webs that are shaped like triangles. Some webs do not have special shapes.

Some spiders dig holes in the ground. These holes are called burrows. Spiders live in the burrows. Some line the burrows with silk. Others make silk doors to cover the burrows.

Some spiders do not make homes. They wander around looking for food. They may spend time in trees or on the ground. Sometimes they hide under plants.

Some spiders make webs for homes.

Silk

Some spiders use silk to build webs. They spin webs to catch prey. Prey is an animal that is hunted by another animal for food. Prey becomes trapped in the sticky silk. Spiders can feel prey move when it is caught in their webs.

Sometimes spiders eat the prey right away. Sometimes spiders wrap their prey in silk. They may eat the prey later.

Most spiders also use silk to move. Some spiders use silk to balloon. Ballooning is floating through the air on a string of silk. Spiders let out a string of silk. Then the wind carries them to different places. Most spiders use silk to drop down from places. Some swing from one place to another.

Spiders can use silk to stay safe. Spiders let out a string of silk when they move. They can quickly go up the string to escape danger.

Some spiders use silk webs to catch prey.

Hunting

Spiders hunt for food. They hunt their prey in several ways.

The trapdoor spider digs a small hole in the ground. This is called a burrow. The spider covers its burrow with a silk door. An insect walks near the trapdoor. The spider senses the insect moving. Then the spider pops out of its burrow. It grabs the insect and hurries inside to eat a meal.

The fishing spider sits on the surface of water. It catches insects that are on the surface. Fishing spiders may eat small fish. The spider dives into the water to escape from predators.

The jumping spider leaps 50 times its body length. The spider jumps on prey and eats it.

The spitting spider spits on its prey. The spit is a sticky glue. It comes out from the spider's fangs. The spit traps the prey. The spider then has a meal.

The trapdoor spider covers its burrow with a silk door.

Eating and Enemies

Spiders catch their food in many ways. But they all eat the same way. Spiders release poison into their prey through their fangs. This poison slows down or kills the prey. Then the spider can eat easily.

Spiders release digestive juices into insects. Digestive juices are juices that break down food. The juices turn insects' insides into liquid. Spiders drink this liquid. Then spiders leave the insects' empty shells behind.

Spiders need to watch out for certain animals. Some lizards and wasps eat spiders. Large spiders may attack small spiders.

Sometimes spiders use camouflage to defend themselves. Camouflage is coloring that makes something look like its surroundings. Some spiders can change colors. This makes the spiders hard to see.

Spiders release poison into their prey through their fangs.

Young Spiders

Mating can be dangerous for some male spiders. Female spiders are often larger than the males. After mating, some females may attack and eat the males.

Many spiders mate in the summer or fall. Some mate anytime. Female spiders make an eggsac out of silk. An eggsac keeps eggs safe. Then they lay their eggs in the eggsac. Some spiders lay only a few eggs. Many lay several hundred. Others lay as many as 1,000 eggs.

Young spiders are called spiderlings. Spiderlings are very small. Some females care for their young. Other spiderlings are on their own. Some balloon away right after hatching.

As spiders grow, they shed their outer shell. This is called molting. Some spiders molt three times before they are fully grown. Others molt as many as 20 times. Some spiders live for about one year. Others live for two or three years. Some spiders live as long as 30 years.

Spiderlings hatch out of eggsacs.

Spiders and People

Many people are afraid of spiders. But only a few spiders can be dangerous to people. In North America, only two kinds of spiders can hurt people. They are the widow and the recluse.

These spiders can be easy for people to spot. Some widows have red marks on their abdomen. Some recluse spiders have violin-shaped marks on their cephalothorax. Other widows and recluses are harder to spot.

People do not need to be afraid of spiders. Spiders help people. Spiders help control the number of insects in the world. They eat insects that carry illnesses and destroy crops. Spiders also help keep gardens free of insects. They kill insects in people's homes, too.

Some widow spiders have red marks on their abdomens.

Hands On: Spider Art

Many people think spiders' webs are beautiful. Now you can turn a spider's web into art.

What You Need

A piece of black paper   Glue   Scissors
A spray can of varnish   A spray can of paint

What You Do

1. Find an adult to help you.
2. Find a spider web outside. Make sure the spider has finished building the web. Also make sure the spider is not on the web.
3. Carefully spray the web with the paint. Gold or white paint works especially well.
4. Spread a thin coat of glue on the black paper.
5. Move the glue side of the paper up against the painted web. Avoid sideways movement. Try to get all parts of the web to stick at the same time.
6. Gently cut the supporting edges of the web.
7. Spray the paper and the web with varnish.

You can hang the spider web in your room. You now have a piece of spider art.

Words to Know

abdomen (AB-duh-muhn)—the large, round back portion of a spider's body; silk is produced here.

arthropod (AR-thruh-pod)—an animal with a hard outer shell and many legs with joints

cephalothorax (seh-fuh-luh-THOR-aks)—the front part of a spider's body; it contains the eyes, mouth, jaws, and legs.

molt (MOHLT)—to shed an outer shell

predator (PRED-uh-tur)—an animal that hunts other animals for food

spiderling (SPYE-dur-ling)—a young spider

spinnerets (spin-uh-RETTS)—holes in a spider's abdomen; silk comes out of them.

Read More

Bender, Lionel. *Spiders*. New York: Gloucester Press, 1988.

Patent, Dorothy Hinshaw. *The Lives of Spiders*. New York: Holiday House, 1980.

Useful Addresses

The American Tarantula Society
P.O. Box 1617
Artesia, NM 88211-1617

Central California Arachnid Society
4082 North Benedict #104
Fresno, CA 93722-4559

Internet Sites

AntBoy's BugWorld
http://www.heatersworld.com/bugworld/spiders.html
Spider Homepage
http://www.powerup.com.au/~glen/spider.htm
The Spider Site
http://www.xs4all.nl/~ednieuw/

Index